ParentSmart Books™

Your Baby and Child's

Growth and Development

Penny A. Shore

with

The International Advisory Council on Parenting

Penelope Leach, Ph.D.

William Sears, M.D.

Martha Sears, R.N.

Otto Weininger, Ph.D.

Canadian Cataloguing in Publication Data

Shore, Penny A.
Your baby & child's growth & development

ISBN 1-896833-14-4

Includes index. 1. Children - Growth. 2. Child development. I. International Advisory Council on
Parenting. II. Title. III. Title: Your baby and child's growth and development. IV. Series: Shore, Penny A.
Parent**Smart** Books.

HQ767.9.S52 2002   649'.1   C2001-901959-9

Published by The Parent Kit Corporation
2 Bloor Street West, Suite 1720
Toronto, Ontario M4W 3E2

Printed in Canada, by St. Joseph Printing Ltd.
First printing November 2001

1 2 3 4 5   05 04 03 02 01

ParentSmart Books
introduction to the series

P arenting has been my passion ever since the day my first child was born. This was, without doubt, an exhilarating and exciting event. However, it didn't take long to realize that with the birth of our child, we were taking on one of the most important jobs in life – and one for which we hadn't taken a training course. Furthermore, the baby didn't come with an instruction manual!

Now, my children have grown into happy, successful young adults and although my job is educational publishing, I have always considered parenting to be my most satisfying career. About four years ago, it occurred to me that I could combine my passion for parenting with my publishing experience. The idea was to produce a series of books designed to give new parents the very help and guidance I was looking for as a new parent. To develop the content, four of the world's leading parenting authorities were recruited to join me in establishing The International Advisory Council on Parenting. The members are; Penelope Leach, Ph.D., Otto Weininger, Ph.D., William Sears, M.D. and Martha Sears, R.N. The result of our combined efforts is the Parent**Smart** book series.

Despite the daily challenges faced by parents, there is probably no job in the world that matches parenting in terms of personal fulfillment and truly wonderful fringe benefits.

Parents who are properly prepared with the right tools and skills will have less stress and are likely to be more effective. That's why each book in the Parent**Smart** book series deals with one particular aspect of parenting. Taken together, the first six books in the series combine to provide a virtual "Parenting 101" course.

These books are unique in many ways. They provide you with a combination of expert information, interactive exercises and journals where you can record important information about your child. By having the full series available in your home, you will have easy access to the knowledge and support you will need to confidently handle most parenting situations.

There is another feature of the Parent**Smart** series that is very special. The experts don't necessarily agree on all parenting issues, and this can be confusing to parents who want their child to benefit from the best advice. We resolved this by having all members of The International Advisory Council on Parenting approve and come to consensus on the content.

A complete list of the other titles in this series, and a description of their contents, can be found at the back of this book. Parent**Smart** books are also a good refresher and primer for new grandparents, child caretakers and others in your extended family who will interact with your child.

Try to complete the questionnaires and exercises when you can. This will help you and your parenting partner to have a basis for communicating on the important issues and to be a better parenting team. The journals will provide records that you can enjoy and share with your children when they are older. "Tips and Techniques" are highlighted in the book to help you make immediate use of your new skills in every day situations.

I hope this book will raise your awareness about important parenting issues and give you the confidence to be a more effective and nurturing parent. Nothing can match the pleasure and happiness of seeing your children grow into fulfilled adults who are getting the best from their lives and whose friendship you cherish.

It has now been well-established that investing in your child's first three years will pay dividends in determining his or her future development. So, good luck with this stage and may your parenting adventure be one of the most rewarding experiences of your lifetime.

Penny Shore

dedication

To Joan, Eric, Jay and Amanda —
from whom I continue to learn.

Your Baby and Child's
Growth and Development

Table of Contents

The Journey of a thousand miles begins with One Step.

Lao·Tsu

growth and development

introduction

From the moment of conception, your child's rate of growth and development is determined by a complex combination of genetic and environmental factors. Growth patterns, established in the genes, will determine his final adult characteristics such as height, shape and proportions.

But it's not always a smooth and steady pattern. Like a rocket that constantly readjusts to remain on a "trajectory" or set path, your child will grow in fits and starts. Along the way, his healthy growth and development also depend on the nourishing food and loving care provided by his caregivers. Environmental influences like serious illnesses and long-term emotional problems are factors that can affect this growth pattern.

Your child's growth and development is a constant reminder of the wonders of nature. But it can also be a source of misplaced concern and competitiveness among parents. That's why it's important for you to understand this rapid and ever-changing growth process.

Over these critical early years, your child's total development is integrated and interdependent. The physical, emotional and intellectual aspects of his growth and development are directly linked. For example, learning to walk doesn't involve only the development of motor skills. With his eyes raised to a new level and his hands free to manipulate and examine things, your walking child now has an opportunity to learn and discover – a new way to interact with the world around him.

Note: *Alternating between feminine and masculine gender in text can be confusing. So, for the sake of clarity, this book will use "he." The information applies equally to boys and girls unless otherwise specified.*

essentials of growth and development

T here are three concepts that you need to understand concerning your child's growth and development.

Your child's growth is "programmed" in him.

Your child's rate of growth and development is largely preset. Your baby's birth weight is his personal starting point, but he will grow after that at roughly the same rate as all other children. Boys tend to be heavier than girls. And statistically, babies of Asian descent are smaller than the Caucasian average, whereas North American babies of African descent tend to be larger. Parents of multiples may also find that even those born at full-term will be on the small side.

Children who are born prematurely did not grow to their optimum weight before birth. As a result, many parents of "preemies" note a phenomenon called "catch-up growth." This means that a premature child may gain at a much faster weekly rate (up to double) than what is expected at certain ages. He is likely to go on gaining weight quickly until he has reached the weight he would have been if his pre-birth growth had been optimal. At this point, his growth rate will slow and then will settle at the rate appropriate to him.

Putting these and other factors aside, all healthy children follow a general rate of growth. If you provide him with the proper nutrition and tender attention – and depending on how his body copes with illness and trauma – your child's growth will follow its programmed course.

Physical development is a process, not a race.

All babies follow the same pattern of physical development, but each one develops at his own, unique rate. So while all babies' muscle control starts at the top and works downward from the neck, shoulders, back and legs, there is no specific age at which each new development will occur. Similarly, milestones like learning to roll, sit, crawl, stand and walk all occur in this order, but you can't predict when they will happen. Babies can't dance before they can walk, just as they can't walk before they stand. How long your child will spend at each of these phases is something no one can predict.

Adopt the pace of nature. Her secret is patience.

RALPH WALDO EMERSON

When your child reaches a specific milestone says nothing about his overall health and well-being, his likelihood of later success or his worth. Simply put, sooner isn't necessarily better. Many parents behave as if the child who walks earlier than the average – well before his peers – will somehow be faster and more physically adept years later. Research has shown that this just isn't so. If your child develops in some way more slowly than his peers, the disappointment you may feel will be communicated to your child, and this more than anything else can impede his progress by damaging his burgeoning self-esteem.

You don't have to "motivate" your child – he will do what he needs to do when he is ready.

Instead of being concerned with your child doing what you want him to do, for example, sitting up or crawling before he is ready, you need to learn from watching what he is trying to do. You can then create a suitably supportive, loving and flexible world for him to grow and learn in. You can help by arranging his environment – or his position in it – so that he can attempt to do what he wants to safely and with confidence. If you watch his cues, your child will show you what he wants to try.

Children learn when they do something that is their own idea, not yours. For example, your baby learns nothing if you stick a rattle in his hand if he's not ready or able to grasp it. He will hear its sound briefly before it falls from his hand. He may be interested in the rattle's sound when you shake it for him, and if so, then this is age-appropriate for him. When his active grasping skills (which are different from the grasp reflex that allows him to hold it momentarily) are developed, he will hold the rattle and begin to discover the noise he can make when he shakes his hand.

POINTS TO REMEMBER

- Your child's growth will follow its programmed course.

- All babies follow the same pattern of physical development, but each one develops at his own, unique rate.

measuring your child's growth on centile charts

Growth and development involve your baby's whole body. While it is not possible for you to measure the growth of bones and internal organs, it's very important to monitor his height if you are going to monitor his weight. Weight gain alone cannot give you a reliable means for tracking your child's growth, since this might indicate a child who is growing fat or heavier, but not larger or longer.

The most useful way to keep track of your child's growth is through the use of standardized centile charts. Based on extensive research surveys of children of all backgrounds, sizes and shapes, the curves provided on centile charts show children's expected weight and height growth rates throughout their growing years.

By plotting your child's weight and height on a centile chart at intervals throughout his early years, you can monitor his growth rate. This way you can check whether your child's weight gains match his height increases and whether his overall growth is at an expected rate. There will be natural variations in the way he grows, so don't be disturbed by some unevenness in his growth pattern.

To keep track of your baby's growth, you can plot his length and weight on the charts provided on pages 88-91. By joining the dots you plot, you will be able to see whether your child's development is within the normal range of the centile lines for his age. On the other hand, if his weight gain falls and remains down, resulting in a new curve at a lower level, he is not growing as he should be. This may be due to illness or not enough nourishment, and you may want to check with his doctor.

Length changes more slowly than weight and is more difficult to measure accurately. Your baby will gain around three-quarters of an inch each month and just over two inches in three months. In order to have a complete record of your child's growth, both weight and height must be charted together.

For most babies, the growth rates shown by the curves on the sample centile charts which follow will be the norm for the first years although there are exceptions, for example, babies who are ill in their first weeks and premature babies.

Note: *Please refer to the growth charts provided on pages 88-91 to plot your child's growth curve.*

POINTS TO REMEMBER

- Your child's growth and development is "programmed" in him.

- Your baby's muscle control starts from the top and works its way down.

- With your support and encouragement, your child will do what he needs to do when he is ready.

the first six months

a whole new world: the newborn experience

For your newborn child, everything – and that means everything – is new. During pregnancy, all of his needs for comfort, warmth, food, oxygen and excreting were taken care of. Suddenly, now that his body is detached from his mother's, he must breathe, suck and swallow food, digest it and rid his system of wastes. His body must convert his food into energy that will enable him to function, stay warm and grow. Lungs that have had no use up to now must breathe to give him oxygen, and he must sneeze and cough to keep his airway clear. On top of all of this, he is bombarded with new stimuli – coolness and warmth on his skin, light and darkness, color, texture, new movements, constraints, hunger, new tastes, fullness and gas. In short, he faces a bewildering array of stimuli to which he must adapt, all in the early months of life. It is no wonder then that a newborn's reactions are unpredictable. How could they be otherwise?

Your child's behavior in these early stages is based on instinct and reflex – his "programming," you might say. For instance, your newborn does not know you are his mother or father. He is programmed to key on human faces, and pay attention to them. He is programmed to suck when offered a nipple. For a newborn, this is part of his essential survival kit.

However much you know about children in general, you don't yet know about this one in particular. You are starting from scratch with every child. You don't know how he will react to being unhappy or hungry or uncomfortable. You don't know exactly what his crying means. All you can do is watch and learn all you can, and have faith in yourself and your desire to do what is best. Your newborn is a bundle to be wrapped and cuddled gently and warmly. Feed him when he seems hungry, talk to him and keep him clean. Most of all, let him come to an understanding of this new world at his own pace and with your support. By observing his responses, you will soon learn what he needs. If something you do seems to distress him, stop it. And if something calms and makes him happy, you've done the right thing.

Tips and techniques for breastfeeding your baby

- A mother's breast milk is perfect for her baby. Begin breastfeeding as soon as possible after your baby is born.

- Let your baby set the schedule and feed him when he is hungry. Note: premature or sick babies will probably not tell you when they are hungry.

- Respond to your baby's cues. Duration and frequency of breastfeeding change. As your baby grows and requires extra milk, by nursing, more milk will be produced to allow for the extra growth.

- Make sure that you and your baby are comfortable during the feeding time. Support your arm with pillows on a comfortable chair, and hold your baby securely in a "cradle hold," so that he is lying on his side in a straight line, with your forearm under his head and your hand under his bottom or legs.

- Skin-to-skin contact with your baby when breastfeeding helps to stimulate both his attention and your milk supply.

- Breastfeed your baby from alternate breasts at successive feedings or from both breasts at one sitting. If breasts are emptied during feeding, adequate milk will be produced.

- Your newborn does not need supplemental feedings of water or juice. He'll get all the fluids he needs from your breast milk.

- Check with your doctor about the effect of caffeine, alcohol intake or any medication in your breast milk. Eat nutritiously to ensure your own energy and your baby's nutrients.

- Even if it seems difficult at first, don't give up. It takes a while to establish breastfeeding. Get support if you experience problems, for example, contact the La Leche League, breastfeeding clinics, or talk to other breastfeeding mothers.

feeding your baby

During the first six months, babies eat a lot because they grow a lot. Feeding your new baby is not only very important, it can also be an intimate and rewarding experience. Try to create healthy attitudes in your child toward food, appetite and eating, while making sure he's getting good nourishment.

It all starts with newborn nursing, by responding to his changing nutritional needs, making good feeding decisions with your parenting partner and getting the support you need to maintain those decisions.

Babies are born with sucking and rooting reflexes that help to ensure that they will be nourished. Feed your baby when he is hungry, establish a two-way communication around feedings and learn your baby's unique signals to you. This may be in the form of crying when he is hungry or body language, such as pulling away when he is full.

One of the very first decisions you'll make is whether to breastfeed or bottlefeed. Babies can survive on breast milk or formula for the first six months – but there is no question that breast milk is best. It is convenient and economical. It is the most complete food you can offer to your baby and provides protection against infections; it is safe, easy to digest and it is nutritionally balanced for your individual baby. As well, breastfeeding is good for the mother's body too. Breastfeeding helps a mother get back into shape after pregnancy and reduces the risk of breast cancer.

Enjoy the intimate cuddling time when feeding your baby. Breastfeeding is a way of uniquely bonding with your infant. If your decision is to bottlefeed your newborn or wean a breastfeeding baby to formula, fathers can also enjoy feeding their baby and give moms a much needed break.

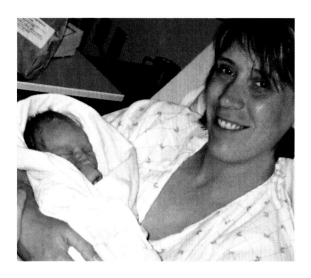

Ask your child what he wants for dinner only if he's buying.

FRAN LEBOWITZ

TIPS and techniques for bottlefeeding your baby

- Make sure that the bottles and nipples are sterilized carefully and follow instructions for formula preparation precisely.

- Use only commercial iron-fortified infant formula for your newborn; never cow's milk. Ask your doctor to recommend an appropriate formula.

- Always refrigerate prepared formula.

- Do not microwave the formula – it heats unevenly. Use a pan of hot water and make sure to test the temperature on the inside of your wrist. Warm the bottle of formula to at least room temperature.

- Check the size of the nipple hole. Formula should drip evenly from the nipple at one-second intervals.

- Burp your baby regularly when he is feeding and follow his cues. He will let you know when he's full.

- If you are weaning a baby from breast to bottle-feeding, allow a week or more for the baby to learn to adjust to the bottle while you are still readily available. You may need to experiment with different types of bottle nipples to find one that he likes.

weight gain

Your baby's birth weight is his personal starting point for growth. Following an initial dip and recovery in weight over the first 10 days, he will gain at roughly the same rate and pace as all other babies. If your baby has six to eight wet diapers a day after the first week and is gaining weight, he is getting adequate food. But it is not a smooth and steady pattern. He may gain seven ounces one week and only three the next, which is why it is important to plot your child's weight on your centile chart.

Your child may gain about two inches in length in the first three months. Since this is a relatively small increment, it is difficult to get accurate measurements. Still, it's important that you periodically record his increases in length so you can monitor weight change in relation to height.

physical development

A newborn's head is so large and heavy in proportion to the rest of him that it acts like a central point toward which his body seems to curl. Until the stage when his body grows so that his head becomes relatively lighter and he gains some strength in his neck, your baby's voluntary movements are limited. He may practice lifting his head away from your shoulder and will always try to turn his head to avoid the danger of smothering, but he has little other control. For the first few weeks, while his neck muscles grow noticeably stronger, he needs your constant support.

By about six weeks, your baby's neck muscles may be strong enough to keep his head upright when he is stationary, though his unsupported head would still flop as you walk or when you put him down and pick him up. Keep your hand at the back of his neck to give him that extra support.

Over the next six weeks or so, your baby's shoulder muscles begin to firm up and the rest of his body will begin to grow more in proportion to his head. By about three months, he may have control of his head and you need only support it with your hand when you pick him up, set him down or move unexpectedly. As his head control improves, his posture will also change. He will no longer curl up as he did when he was a newborn; he will now lie back with his arms and legs waving freely. When placed on his stomach, he may lift his head and look around – an important change that will offer him new perspectives on the world. Now he can look around at what interests him and enjoy toys and mobiles, and he will begin to play with his arms and legs. This is the beginning of the joy of physical play and the fun of learning to use his body.

safety alert

One reflex, called the Moro Response, is a baby's reaction to his sense that he is about to be dropped. If you let your baby's head go back or you put him down too quickly and begin to pull your hands away before he feels securely at rest, he will throw out his arms and legs, then clutch reflexively at nothing and likely cry out in fear. This is a sign that you have handled him too roughly, too suddenly or without sufficient support for his head and that you must take more care.

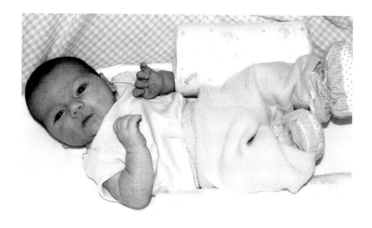

Sometime after six weeks, he may move constantly when awake, waving his hands and kicking. His feet describe a smooth circular motion like riding a bike, very different from the jerky movements of the newborn. And as his hand movements become more controlled, he'll begin to play with his hands. Around eight weeks, he may discover that these are his hands and he can control them.

By three months, or soon after, your baby may have sufficient muscle control to roll from his back to his side. Think of what this means for him. By rolling or lifting his head to see something new, your baby can now change his perspective, watch his feet and hands, and engage them in play. Fascinated by the world and his newfound ability to simply gaze around, he'll enjoy being free of constraining blankets in surroundings that are bright and interesting.

Between three and four months, as his back muscles develop, your baby may begin to enjoy being propped in a sitting position. Now strong enough to hold up his head and shoulders, he won't droop forward with his head to his knees. A favorite game for both of you may be for him to grasp your fingers and pull himself up to a sitting position. He'll want to play the pulling-to-sitting game (let him do the pulling) over and over. When propping him up, take care to give him adequate support with pillows or a baby seat so he doesn't slide down. The ideal way to do this is to use a fabric bouncing chair or adjustable baby seat that can be set at different angles as his posture changes. Use one that is equipped with a belt that goes around the waist and between his legs – it will keep him safe and comfortable.

With the new strength in his neck, shoulders and arms, your baby may soon learn to prop himself up on his arms when you put him on his stomach. A few weeks later, he may be pulling up his legs from underneath him and moving onto his knees or even onto his feet. But even when he has mastered the individual techniques required to organize each end of his body, he isn't likely to be able to coordinate these two actions and get his stomach off the floor. It may still be a long time before he can actually crawl.

---

safety alert

The ability to roll means that your baby may be able to propel himself off the change table or other surfaces that have been relatively safe until now. Time for a little extra vigilance on your part! Stay close when he is on the change table or any surface that he could roll off.

---

sleep and your newborn

While your newborn may sleep for two-thirds or more of the day, there are no predictable sleep patterns. Every baby has his own individual sleep rhythm, determined by his unique physical needs. Babies' sleeping periods are much shorter than adults', with more light than deep sleep, and more night waking.

Babies tend to sleep for approximately one to three hours and then have a wakeful period of about half an hour. Breastfed babies may wake to feed more often than bottlefed babies, as breast milk digests more quickly. A newborn will not know day from night, and you can not force a baby to sleep. You can, however, create an environment that is more conducive to allowing for your infant's sleep. Babies awaken easily in the early months, so that they can signal their needs to us, for example, hunger

or a need for warmth. This frequent waking stage will not last forever. Your baby's sleep habits are more determined by his temperament than your parenting abilities. The most important factor in helping your baby to develop healthy sleep habits is to establish predictable, consistent bedtime routines.

Not many babies sleep through the night before six months. There is no right or wrong way to approach helping your baby's sleep – different techniques work at different developmental stages and every baby has individual needs. Try part of one strategy and part of another to see what works, and use your baby as the indicator. Develop a nighttime parenting style that works for you and your baby – with the goal that your waking baby will be able to soothe *himself* to sleep.

---

safety alert

Research conducted in several countries suggests that letting your baby sleep on his back will reduce the risk of Sudden Infant Death Syndrome (SIDS), also known as crib death. Other recommendations include breastfeeding, stopping smoking during pregnancy or exposing your baby to second-hand smoke after birth, and avoiding dressing your baby too warmly.

- **If your baby is using a crib, make sure it is one approved after the new safety requirements.**
- **Make your baby's sleeping arrangements safe. If using a crib, position it away from light switches, dangling cords or other dangerous items the baby might reach.**
- **Pillows should not be used in a crib, as there could be a risk of smothering.**

TIPS and techniques for baby's sleeptime

Remember to choose techniques that are appropriate for your baby's age, stage and temperament and that suit your own lifestyle and sleep habits.

- Wait until your baby is tired before putting him to bed.

- Wrap your newborn or "swaddle" securely at bedtime, but make sure the wrapping is appropriate for the room temperature. Older babies settle better in looser coverings.

- Try sounds which might soothe the baby. Although most babies can block out disturbing noises, some babies need a quieter sleeping environment. White noise, such as a running fan or humidifier, blocks out other sounds. Make your own tape of sounds and songs that work – maybe even your own voice softly singing.

- Holding and closeness during the day with your baby may promote calmness and carry over into nighttime calmness. The warmth and comfort of your body, while breast or bottlefeeding your baby, induces sleep.

- Feeding your baby on cue during the day may promote better sleep at night.

- Try to go to your baby quickly if he cries. If he's not hungry, you may be able to settle him back to sleep before he wakes completely. The warm, gentle touch of your hands on your baby's body may induce him to fall back to sleep.

- Sleeping with your baby in your bed works for some families, and can have benefits especially for a breastfeeding mother.

- "Wear your baby" in a baby sling or snugly and walk with him until he calms down.

- A massage or warm bath is relaxing for both your baby and you.

- Rock, cuddle or nestle your baby until you are certain that he is sound asleep. Eventually, he may be able to soothe himself to sleep.

- Avoid waking your lightly sleeping baby – watch for signs of limp limbs and a motionless face to make sure that your baby is in a deep sleep stage before moving away.

- Try to have consistent bedtimes and rituals such as stories and songs for older babies.

getting to know you

Your baby's prime need is for people, although, of course, he doesn't know what "people" means. In the earliest stages, he simply gives full visual attention to anything "face-like" and listens intently to anything "voice-like." New babies are programmed to react to faces, and if you watch him looking at yours, you'll see his gaze begin at the top, scan the hairline, move slowly down to the chin and then back to the eyes. Once he has located your eyes, he may hold his gaze longer than he would on anything else. Somewhere from three to eight weeks, when he has learned enough about faces, your baby will respond – with a smile.

When your baby smiles, which causes many parents to melt, it may look like love and it soon will be. At the earliest stages, it is intuitive, a protection against neglect by creating a pleasant interchange with others. The more he smiles and gurgles, the more people will smile and talk to him. And the more attention people give him, the more he will respond. A cycle of positive interplay has begun.

It is through this interaction with adults who find him appealing and who, therefore, give him attention, that he will be able to learn and recognize particular faces. Around 12 weeks, it may be clear that he knows you. While he still smiles at most everyone, he will save the biggest, happiest smile for those he knows best, for those people who come when he needs help or company, who react to his smiles and smile back, who listen to his "talk" and talk back.

CASE STUDY 1

Rebecca takes her five-month-old baby, Andrew, with her everywhere she goes. At first she had been puzzled by his changing moods – he would laugh and coo at the grocery store one visit and be cranky and unsettled the next. It was about Andrew's third month that Rebecca began to recognize the signals that he was sending out. By now she could recognize when he was tired (and a trip to the store was ill-advised) because he would tug at his earlobe and seem unhappy no matter what she did. Instead of taking him out for some new diversion, Rebecca knew it was best to let him settle in for a nap or at least for a little quiet time. Rebecca was also able to read Andrew's other cues that signaled he was overstimulated, hungry or not feeling well. She realized that though Andrew couldn't tell her what he was feeling, he was able to show her. By being aware of the non-verbal cues he was giving out, Rebecca was able to give him what he needed when he needed it.

first conversations

It may be quite early – sometime in the second month –
when your baby begins to associate listening with looking.
You'll notice one day when you speak that your child
suddenly starts looking about trying to find the source
of your voice. It is because of this intuitive interest
in listening to people's voices that most babies' first
deliberate sounds happen in some sort of social situation –
like playing with an adult. Unlike the gurgles after feeding
and whimpers just before a crying jag, the sounds that
accompany smiles are not incidental. These sounds are
deliberate, though not in the sense that he is trying to say
something specific. Instead, he is using his voice as a
means of interacting with you.

Notice that when you say something to your baby, he'll say
something back and then pause as if waiting for a reply.
When you say something more, he'll wait until you finish
and then make some more noises. Studies have shown
that noises other than a voice do not encourage him to
respond this way. Your baby is "answering" because some-
one is talking to him, not just because he hears a sound.

> It is important to admit
> from the outset that,
> whereas babies are the
> creation of two people, they are
> themselves third parties,
> independent
> even if indebted,
> isolated even if protected.
>
> PETER USTINOV

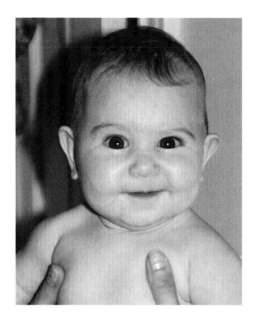

Babies who are talked to a great deal are, not surprisingly, talkative. Babies who get less "conversation," who are not handled much at all or who are usually competing with an older child's demand for adult attention may "talk" less.

Of course, babies don't just talk when they are spoken to. They also talk on their own, in the crib, in the stroller, anywhere. Even this "chat" has a conversational tone to it, replete with noises followed by pauses, then more noises and so on. Interestingly, babies who talk a lot are likely to be more contented when alone than less chatty babies. As he practices, he will begin to coo and babble for a few months, almost like he is offering a running commentary on the excitement and stimulation he is beginning to thrive on. He is not really talking, of course – he won't begin to try to make words until around one year – though parents are often tempted to try to identify words. The ease and fluency with which your baby babbles at six months is closely related to the facility with which he will learn to use real language later on. His talkativeness now is partly dependent on adults talking to him. If you find that simply chatting away with your baby makes you feel silly or self-conscious, you might like to try the techniques on the following page.

- Look at books together. Point to and name the things shown on the pages and tell your baby – just as you would a much older child – what is going on. He won't understand, but he will enjoy the pictures and your voice.

- Talk about what you are doing as you do it – whether it is a bath, a diaper change or a feeding. Give the names of objects around your home and explanations for your actions – for example, "Here's juice for Matthew." and "I'm watering the plant now."

- Create a conversation. Ask questions like, "Shall we go out for a walk today?" He won't answer in words, of course, but he will respond with conversational tones and gestures.

- Talk naturally. He needs to hear normal tones, not stilted or oversimplified talk.

- Listen to your baby. Try to answer him in words when he makes noises to you. He is not looking for a monologue in which you hold forth. What he's after is a little "conversation" – for example, "So, you're ready for your lunch now."

POINTS TO REMEMBER

- Your child's behavior in the early months of life is based on instinct and reflex.

- Watch and learn all you can. Have faith in yourself and your desire to do what is best.

- Respond to your baby's unique feeding cues and signals to you.

- Every baby has an individual sleep rhythm, determined by his unique physical needs.

- Your baby first uses his voice sounds as a means of interacting with you.

We need four hugs a day for survival. We need eight hugs a day for maintenance. We need twelve hugs a day for growth.

VIRGINIA SATIR

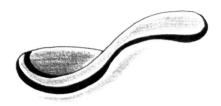

from six months to one year

By approximately six months, your child may begin to delight in his body and what it will do, whether he is trying to roll over, trying to balance in the sitting position or trying to get up on all fours. He is beginning to understand how all these different parts of his body can work together. It is an exciting time for him.

starting baby on solid foods

Breastfeeding for at least six months or more is good for your baby. Although most babies appear to become interested in solid foods at around six months, others are still quite content to take only breast or formula feedings. If leaving solids until six months, parents should be aware of possible iron deficiency. Your family doctor may recommend a daily dose of multivitamin drops to ensure that your baby is receiving his required nourishment.

Babies' feeding requirements vary, depending on their rates of development and appetites. One indicator is, if your baby has doubled his birth weight or weighs approximately 12 to 13 pounds, he is probably ready for solid foods. Look for signs of your child's readiness to try solid foods. Things to look for include: hunger after feedings, wanting night feedings he had abandoned earlier, chewing motions, intent interest in your food or poor weight gain. He should be able to sit with your help. Observing these signs will help you to decide when he is ready to add solids to his feedings.

Most experts advise not to introduce solids before four to six months. Your child can better digest solids by six months. Using a small spoon, start gradually with an iron-fortified rice cereal – one teaspoon once or twice a day, mixed quite thinly with breast milk, formula or water.

Gradually increase his solids by adding other cereals, puréed fruit and then vegetables. Prepared baby foods are fully cooked. Check instructions on labels for serving and storing. Wait five to seven days in between each new food you introduce to see if he is sensitive or allergic to any of them. Try to introduce any new foods in the morning to watch for allergic reactions, such as coughing, runny nose, wheezing, vomiting, diarrhea or a rash. Don't be in a hurry to wean your baby from the breast or bottle. Breast milk is still the nutritionally superior food, so take care that solid foods do not replace your baby's milk intake. Solids should not substitute but rather complement his feedings, as your baby shows interest.

By introducing nutritious solids gradually, in a relaxed atmosphere, you can begin to build your child's healthy attitude toward eating. Both you and your baby can share this feeding time together. Talk to your baby about the food and what you are doing, for example, "Sammy, here is some banana, would you like to taste it?"

Introduce new tastes and textures like puréed carrots, mashed potatoes and teething biscuits so that he can learn to chew and swallow. Until nine months, breast or formula milk is still very important, with solids offered as an "extra." At this stage, he even may be ready for bite-sized vegetables, poultry, cheese and yogurt, as his self-feeding skills improve. Never force your child to eat; it creates negative feelings about eating. For his healthy development, it's important to keep feeding experiences positive, social and enjoyable.

Tips and techniques for introducing solid foods to your baby

- Watch for signs of your baby's readiness for solid foods at around six months.

- Introduce solids gradually to watch for allergic reactions. Add one new food at a time (wait five to seven days in between each new food introduced) before introducing another. Start with one teaspoon at a time.

- By keeping connected to and "reading" your baby, you will know when he is hungry. Do not force-feed your baby.

- Make feedings a relaxed and loving time for your baby to experience the enjoyment of food and the time together.

- Seal food and store in the refrigerator.

- Have your baby's high chair in an easily cleaned space and encourage self-feeding especially with his fingers. This may be messy as your baby tries to put the spoon in his mouth, but eventually he will master his feeding skills.

- You can switch your baby to chunkier baby foods, new textures and tastes between seven and nine months. Make sure any pieces of food are small, chewable and digestible.

weight gain

Between the ages of six months and one year, your baby's rate of growth slows down. Don't expect more than two to three ounces per week with an overall height increase of two to three inches. If you are tracking your baby's weight gain on the centile chart, you'll see that a slower rate of growth follows the general trend of the curve.

physical development

About halfway through his first year, your baby's control of his muscles may be halfway between his head and his feet – at the lower back level. He is likely, or soon will be able, to balance himself in a sitting position for a few seconds. Remember, though, that he cannot get himself into the sitting position; that's your job. Place him squarely on his bottom, splay his legs in front of him for balance and slowly release him – but be ready because he will begin to topple soon. Some babies figure out that when they place their hands on the floor in front of them while sitting up, they can balance for an extended period of time. But this isn't a particularly satisfying position since both hands are occupied and, therefore, unavailable for play or sucking. In addition, leaning over in this way limits his ability to look around the room to investigate and interact with other people nearby.

You can free up your baby's hands and help him sit by packing cushions and rolled blankets behind his buttocks and all around to prop him up and also cushion the inevitable tumble. He is programmed to want to sit up, but it may be a while before he can look around or play with something placed in front of him without toppling. Eventually, though, it becomes a wonderfully convenient position for you to engage him in all sorts of mutual play.

It was a late Thursday afternoon in the waiting room of a pediatrician's office. Roberta sat with her eight-month-old, Samuel, while she chatted with another mother, Lisa, and her daughter Emma, seven months old. As the two first-time mothers talked, their babies gurgled and cooed and looked about. Since both mothers were awaiting routine baby checkups, they started to talk about their experiences over the last few months. Both were glad to have the chance to share their feelings and a few laughs with somebody else going through the same stages at the same time. "Don't you love the way you can play together now that he's sitting up?" asked Lisa. Roberta started to answer and then stopped. Samuel wasn't sitting up yet. And he is older, she thought. She felt embarrassed suddenly and flushed. At this moment, the reception-area nurse came and called Roberta in for her appointment.

After the checkup was over and the doctor said everything was okay, Roberta spoke up. "If Samuel truly is fine, then why is a younger baby able to sit up before he is?" The doctor heard the concern and anxiety in Roberta's voice and sat down to discuss it with her. "Samuel is terrific, Roberta. Everything's fine. All babies go through the same development pattern, but they don't all do it at exactly the same age. Sammy will sit up when he is good and ready. The only effect of worrying about all this is that you get worked up and anxious. There is no problem here, so just relax and enjoy your baby."

Roberta was relieved to hear that and, after saying good-bye, she headed out to the waiting room. "So, how did it go?" asked Lisa as they emerged. "Great," said Roberta. The two mothers then exchanged phone numbers so they could stay in touch and offer each other a little mutual support from time to time.

changing sleep patterns

Between six months and a year, there are more wakeful hours where your child is developing new skills and is aware of what is going on around him. He is more responsive to the stimulation provided by his caregivers. Morning and afternoon rests can be a daily routine, even if your baby doesn't sleep. It is important for your baby to have consistent and predictable naptimes, bedtimes, mealtimes and playtimes. A baby who feels more secure will develop healthier sleep habits.

There are techniques that you can use to encourage your baby to sleep through the night. Some parents have their baby sleep with them, while others respond to their night waking child's cries by gently patting or stroking him in his crib, but not picking him up, until he calms down. Other parents simply alternate a good night's sleep with their partner so that exhaustion doesn't take over. Whatever techniques are used, every family's needs are different and every baby is an individual.

Night waking can be caused by a variety of things – teething, heat, cold, a wet diaper or baby going through a developmental stage. Your baby's individual physical needs and temperament play a role in his sleeping patterns. Have a regular bedtime and make sure your baby is sleepy before putting him to bed.

You can create a pleasant, friendly sleeping environment for your baby by making the crib cozy with the addition of soft toys and a cuddly blanket. By having predictable routines and feeling a sense of security, he will adjust more readily to going to sleep – and be able to soothe himself back to sleep if he wakes. Always make sure that he doesn't associate bedtime with punishment. If he does cry, go to him to see what's wrong. You may want to rock, sing or cuddle him back to sleep, but teach your child that night-time is not playtime. Eventually all babies learn to settle themselves and finally sleep through the night.

on the move

Babies need to learn how to sit up alone and must eventually learn to stand and then walk, but how they choose to get around in the interim – if at all – will vary. Some babies learn to crawl at the same time that they learn to support themselves while sitting alone. Others will not crawl before they are one year old. Some may not crawl at all. This, too, is perfectly normal, as these children very often seem more interested in pulling them-selves to a standing position. So while we describe here the usual progress of a child from sitting to walking, there are other equally effective ways for babies to get around.

Among the common alternatives to crawling is "bottom-shuffling." A few babies who have learned to sit up and balance quite early may start to move around on their bottoms, pushing forward with one or two hands. This can be a quick and easy way to get around without the effort of shifting into the crawling position. Some babies who do this will skip crawling altogether.

There is very little you need to do to help your baby crawl, as he can quite easily get himself into the right position either from lying on his stomach or from the sitting position. Rather, no matter how he chooses to get around, your responsibility here is to make sure his environment is a safe one.

If your child does crawl, his development will likely follow this path. By pushing up with his hands and pulling his knees forward, he'll one day find himself in the crawling position with his tummy right off the floor. And while he'll suddenly be in the "correct" crawling position, he will not get anywhere. As you watch him during his seventh and eighth months, you can almost see him "thinking" himself forward. During the latter part of this period, he may rock back and forth, swivel around and, frustrated with his lack of progress across the floor, try rolling, pivoting and squirming on his stomach. While none of these could be called crawling, he is certainly getting himself going.

It's often in the ninth month that babies begin to move by crawling. At first go, however, it may be backward. Because his arms and shoulders are more developed than his lower body, your baby will actually move himself away from where he wants to go. This can be very frustrating – not surprisingly – but he will soon learn what he has to do and will get it right.

safety alert

- Protect your baby's knees by putting him in long pants. Keep him away from rough wood floors where he can pick up splinters.

- Stairs are another obvious danger and must be barricaded. Watch to make sure that his hands don't get pinched in a safety gate.

- With your baby's ability to crawl comes the capacity to get to hazardous objects that up until now have been safely out of harm's way. These include, among others, electrical cords, tablecloths, easily tipped furniture, dangling plants and tiny objects such as pins on the floor.

- Get used to the fact that you cannot leave him alone anymore – he is on the move and will not sit still. Neither should you restrict him in a playpen; he is going through this arduous process to get somewhere, yes, but he is also in a crucial development phase. Impeding him will frustrate him and prevent him from learning what his body can do.

- Finally, let him get dirty. This is his chance to explore and there's no point in being fussy about cleanliness. Ordinary dust won't necessarily hurt him and he'll delight in the chance for a little freedom. Besides, you can wash him up after a good romp.

Fall seven times, stand up eight.

JAPANESE PROVERB

on two feet

At around six months, your baby may love to be held standing on your lap, where he will "jump" by bending and straightening both legs at the same time. Almost every time he finds himself in your lap, your baby may try to turn around to clutch your lapels and pull himself upright. This is an exciting, new talent that enables him to look into your face and over your shoulder to the great world beyond – all at his own instigation. During his seventh month, your baby may begin to jump on alternate legs, creating a dance accompanied by much giggling and laughing.

By approximately 10 months, the downward process of muscular development may have progressed to his knees and feet, allowing him to support his whole weight with some confidence. He won't be able to balance, however, and will need you or a piece of furniture to support him. He may need help sitting down again for several weeks. Rather than picking him up and placing him in a sitting position, help him lower himself down to the floor. This will give him the confidence to eventually plop down by himself.

cruising without a bruising

About a month after pulling himself to a standing position while holding on, your baby may start "cruising" – a sort of walking with the support of the furniture around the room. This usually begins in the crib where he might grip the crib rail and take a few tentative steps sideways as his hands slide along in front of him, before dropping back down. Before long, he will have the confidence to step back slightly and, knowing his legs will support him, move hand-over-hand around the room. Sometime after 12 months, he may be standing almost upright, his arm extended for only occasional balancing.

Don't bother with shoes at this point. If he has shoes on, he will be unable to feel the floor and will have much more trouble balancing. Shoes, or even socks, also tend to be slippery on bare floors, making the effort even more

precarious and will actually undermine his confidence. Bare feet are best, at most, slippers with non-slip soles. He may not enjoy walking holding your hand. At this age, your baby may seem to need the solidity of a sofa or some other large piece of furniture to help him muster the courage for a cruising expedition.

Most importantly, don't hurry the process. Until your baby is sufficiently developed, confident and motivated enough to give it a try, pressuring him to walk before he's ready may cause falls and bruises, which could turn him off the undertaking and slow him in his natural progression. While many children start cruising at about 12 months, some take longer and others start sooner. This wide range is completely normal, and you can be sure your child is standing or cruising because he has discovered something else that gives him a great deal of pleasure.

creating a baby-friendly home

Newly mobile babies aren't always easy to monitor. Suddenly on the move, your child is able as never before to get himself into difficulties and even danger. You have to watch him every minute that he is awake and still give him the freedom to discover and grow, while preserving some semblance of normalcy in the house for the rest of the family. It is no wonder then that some parents have described this stage of development as one of the more challenging times.

Here are a few things you can do that will help you avoid some of the frustrations and make it a more rewarding and fun time.

- **Anticipate.** As a parent, you can find pleasure in being there for your child by anticipating what he needs at precisely that moment. Whether it's a little guidance that's preventive, a clever distraction before a crisis, or the ability to recognize danger before it arises, you can avoid not only some unpleasantness, but you can also reduce the anxiety and stress that invariably results. If there is a particular source of conflict, like the books he loves to pull off the shelves and chew on, remove them. If it is the kitchen cupboard that he loves to pull open, secure it with a childproof latch. The inconvenience that this may cause is preferable to the friction, and even resentment, that could result between you and your baby.

- **Put in place any and all safety precautions at once.** You'll feel much more at ease if you know there is no way that he can burn, cut, electrocute or otherwise harm himself. Safety precautions will really save you as much trouble as they will him.

- **Create positive alternatives to forbidden activities.** If your baby is getting into something he shouldn't be, then it is simply a matter of redirecting his energy and attention to some other interesting activity. Make one kitchen drawer that is "his," and keep all your safe (and noisy, perhaps) implements there. Remember that he has a limited memory and will likely forget any intriguing object only minutes after it has been removed from him – or after he has been removed from it.

- **Learn to live with a little chaos.** Don't even think about keeping your whole home tidy all the time. Your baby will move – now that he can – from activity to activity and will leave a trail of disorder behind him. Instead of scurrying after him cleaning and tidying up, enjoy the activities with him and do a cleanup later on. You may also choose to make certain rooms of the house "playrooms." By doing this, you not only get to play with your baby, you also don't end up spending all your time putting the same things away again and again.

safety alert

- Once your baby has begun to enjoy a certain mobility, he will do almost anything anywhere to repeat a thrill. This means he is more prone to hurt himself. This new activity level will most likely lead to a fall if he happens to be on a bed, chair or sofa. While a minor fall is unlikely to do any real harm, it may unnerve him, and this may reduce his confidence and impede his progress and development.

- Never leave him alone after placing him on the floor surrounded by pillows. He could easily tumble over into an awkward position face down, which makes smothering a real concern.

- His added bulk and new strength mean that lightweight carriages and chairs can easily tip as he struggles to sit up. They should not be used except under constant supervision. Every stroller, high chair and similar baby furniture that you will be using at this point comes equipped with a safety harness. Always use it.

TIPS and techniques for playing games with your baby

- Sit him up with cushions tucked behind his back and his legs apart. Roll a big soft ball – the foam kind is best – so his body traps it. As he dislodges it, it will roll back to you. A new game is born.

- Build a tower between his legs. Then let him knock it down. Build with things that look, feel and sound different – light plastic blocks, foam toys, yogurt containers (but throw these out before they get cracked and sharp).

- Help him discover about pulling things on strings with a pull toy or a string attached to a favorite toy. Place it out of his reach and let him see what happens. He will probably jerk the string accidentally at first, then deliberately.

- Use pots and pans to make noise or show him how to put the lids on.

- Put him on his stomach, lie beside him on yours and demonstrate pushing yourself up, first on your elbows and then on your hands.

- Use various mobiles and play centers for your baby to look at and touch.

- Sit him on your tummy and combine horsey-riding for him with sit-ups and leg-raises for yourself.

- Provide many things for your baby to grasp – in different sizes, colors, shapes and textures.

- Use a towel or blanket to play "hide-the-toy."

- Play peekaboo behind couches and corners.

CASE STUDY 3

Angela was only one year old when she began to walk, but she looked much older. One day at the park, she was playing in the sandbox with a group of older children. Without warning, Angela got to her feet and started to climb out, inadvertently ruining a number of other children's sand castles. While Beth, Angela's mother, intervened to smooth ruffled feathers, one of the other children's parents remarked that this little girl was "old enough to know better." It was only two weeks earlier that Beth found herself being unfair to Angela in just the same way. After Beth spent the better part of a morning washing and polishing the kitchen floor, it was time for Angela's lunch. As soon as she was given her juice, Angela laughingly threw it on the newly waxed floor. Beth reacted with anger and Angela burst into tears. Beth's reaction was similar to the indignant mother's at the park who had assumed that Angela was much older than she really was.

All parents are inclined to make such snap assessments based on appearances, even when dealing with their own children. Somehow, if children are able to walk or talk, then the parents think that these children "must" be able to understand. But it doesn't always work that way. One-year-old Angela didn't know that a puddle of juice in the middle of the kitchen is not a desirable thing. From her perspective, how different is the juice on the kitchen floor from the soapy water and wax that her mother had splashed on the floor just an hour ago? This doesn't mean you won't lose your patience sometimes – for you most assuredly will. But what it does mean is that you have to try to let go of the frustration, anger or stress that you're feeling and recognize that your child will have no idea why you are reacting this way.

Tips and techniques for helping your baby listen and talk

- Talk directly to your baby. He cannot understand general conversation nor distinguish words in the hubbub of family chatter. He needs a "conversation" with you.

- Use key label words. Your baby is going to pick out words that recur in conversation and learn what they mean. Use the word when you are talking to him and use his name, too. For example, say, "Where are Evan's shoes?" instead of "Where are they?" It will mean a lot more to him.

- Let your baby see what you are talking about. Allow him to make a connection between the object and the key word – for example, "Here is Dylan's stroller."

- Talk about things that interest your baby. Remind him of the dog he saw chasing sticks in the park. He may not understand the entire content, but he will grasp what it is you are talking about.

- Use lots of gestures. Point to the things you are talking about and act out stories.

- Be responsive. Try to understand his words. If he points at something and utters a sound, work with him to figure out what he is saying. Try to match his "own-words" to yours. When you make the connection and hit the right word, he will be delighted.

- Help your baby with a few words in key situations. When you are playing roll the ball, use the word "ball." Let him know what you are talking about. The fun he is having with you will help him remember the word.

- Don't correct your baby's words. Correcting him or trying to get him to say it "correctly" will only bore him. Whether it is a mispronunciation or one of his "own-words," the word he uses is the label that he has given the object.

beginning to talk

The time before your child's first birthday is crucial in language development, despite the fact that many children won't produce a single recognizable word before the age of 12 months. Your baby must learn language by listening to it and by learning to understand what it means. The key here is to give him lots to listen to, respond to, and begin to understand. In the middle of his first year, your baby is probably enjoying long, babbling conversations replete with pauses and single-syllable cooing. A month or two later, syllables combine and begin to sound more like words. In addition, he adds more sounds to his repertory, and his "conversation" takes on a whole new, more animated tone. At about eight months, many babies may begin to take interest in adult conversation. Watching intently, looking back and forth to see who is speaking, your child may eventually feel the urge to join in and may do so by shouting for attention. This deliberate intervention is his first use of a speech sound with a specific desire to communicate.

The ninth month – or soon thereafter – usually produces some exciting developments. Your baby's speech may become more elaborate with longer strings of the same syllables as well as new inflections and a different emphasis on sounds. His speech is beginning to resemble yours more as he seems to be exclaiming, asking questions, even making jokes. Later, he may begin mixing different syllables together into apparently long and meaningful "sentences." This kind of chatter, called "jargoning," is a sign that your baby is on the verge of producing real words. There is no real point in trying hard to identify your child's first words. His expressive jargon is your assurance that he will start speaking when he is ready. But it is important that you listen and react to him with adult talk. Being listened to and responded to is what your baby needs most for speech development.

At approximately 11 months, your child may begin applying certain sounds to certain objects, though these may vary at the beginning. These are called "own-words," and they do signify the start of attaching a certain word to a certain object – to language as it were, for example, "baba" for "bottle." It just doesn't happen to be your language. Your baby's likely first use of a word will be something that is exciting or fun for him, perhaps the word "shoe" will tumble out as he tries on a new pair, or he'll blurt out "ball" as you begin to play a game. Don't assume that he is not learning language if the first words come slowly and he has only used one or two. Your baby may be busy learning and beginning to understand the meaning of a dozen words before he actually says one or two.

POINTS TO REMEMBER

- Feeding requirements vary depending on the baby's individual rate of development and appetite.

- Try to introduce new foods to your baby in the morning to watch for any allergic reactions.

- Never force your child to eat. Keep feeding experiences positive, social and enjoyable.

- It is important for your baby to have consistent routines e.g. naptimes and mealtimes.

- Talk directly and responsively to your baby as much as possible using key label words and gestures.

- Once your baby starts moving around, your responsibility is to make sure his environment is safe.

toddler: from one to two-and-a-half

By the time your baby reaches 12 months, his growth is less rapid and his eating patterns are changing. He's now more interested in exploring all the exciting things around him. Toddlers are constantly on the move and don't sit still for long. There are also changes in his emotional and motor development, enabling him to become more independent, even in the area of feeding.

feeding your toddler

At this time, your toddler's tastes, chewing and swallowing skills are more developed. His interest in self-feeding should be encouraged, as it is an important step in his development.

By providing the chance to practice feeding himself, your toddler will develop confidence as he begins to assert his independence. Let him hold the spoon, and offer him finger foods like apple slices, bananas and cooked carrot sticks. At this point, he is ready to share most of the family's food which you can cut up, mince or mash.

Toddlers are so active that they need a number of small meals or nutritious snacks each day. This "grazing" with healthy snacks such as rice cakes and crackers, accompanied by appetizing vegetable dips or puréed fruit, will provide the nutrition your child requires. Your toddler may be hungry one day and not want to eat much the following day. This is normal and usually balances out. While eating, your child should be sitting in a highchair and supervised to prevent choking. Some toddlers can not tolerate being confined for long in a high chair, so you can provide a "nibble tray" on a low level table for easy access.

- Help your child to verbalize his own hunger feelings.

- Respect your child's hunger or fullness.

- Avoid power struggles over food.

- Let your child be part of identifying what he wants to eat.

- Help him to recognize that he should stop eating when he's had enough.

- Offer a healthy balance of food to your child at mealtimes.

weight gain

Once your child is past the age of one year, his weight gain may slow to about one to two ounces per week, though higher or lower rates of weight gain are, as noted earlier in this book, not necessarily a cause for concern. By occasionally checking and updating your child's growth chart, you can keep track of his growth and development.

physical activity and development

At one year, when your child is standing, his proportions appear very different from those of an even slightly older child. His head is still out of proportion to the rest of his body and it sits atop slender shoulders (his neck is barely visible). His chest is too thin, particularly in relation to his round belly. His legs will likely seem bowed and his feet flat. This is a body well suited to getting around on all fours, but one that looks ungainly now that he is upright. Not to worry – his body will now begin to change to keep up with his transition to standing. By approximately age two, he will be much more suitably proportioned for his new posture, and by about three he will begin to be more slender and stretched-out and will have the athletic legginess of a preschooler.

sleeping and your toddler

Although most toddlers sleep between 10 and 12 hours a night, many still wake up one or more times. Teaching your child how to sleep at night without you is a challenge. You want him to settle down happily and easily, but research shows that over half of all children between one and two years make a fuss at bedtime. You need to experiment with different strategies and techniques to see what works best for your family and child.

Daytime naps are suggested for an active child, especially if he isn't sleeping the full 10 to 12 hours at night. Your

toddler needs to be watched for signals of fatigue. His busy day of physical activity, constant learning, excitement or frustration can lead to exhaustion. Your toddler will show signs which indicate that it might be time for a rest or at least some quiet time.

Tips and techniques for toddler naptime

Respect your toddler's individual needs for naps and try the following:

- Make sure your toddler is comfortable. Loosen restrictive clothing and remove shoes.

- Try to have routine times for naps.

- Set the stage for naptime. Close the blinds, turn music or TV off, and speak more quietly.

- Make sure your child is not hungry and that if he's still in diapers, he is dry.

- A back rub may help relax your active toddler and ready him for sleep.

- Fresh air and exercise encourage healthier and longer sleep time.

- If your toddler is a non-napper, a quiet time with some books or a few toys will give him – and you – a refreshing rest.

walking

The progression to walking is a gradual one, based on muscular development and coordination. The important thing to remember is that it really isn't important how early your child begins to stand, cruise or walk, but rather that when he does try, he is comfortable with the attempt. Don't forget that he is busy learning many things right now and may be devoting his energy and attention to different, equally fascinating and important tasks.

Once your child starts cruising, he moves with the help of any convenient support. As his confidence in his ability to stay upright grows, he maintains the contact just for balance. And as his confidence in his balance increases, he will likely rely less and less upon support. One day, confronted by a gap in available support, he will, perhaps even without realizing it, toddle two or three steps, unaided, to his next support object.

For a toddler, walking is an accomplishment in itself; it's not, at first, a means of getting from point A to point B. When you are moving around busily, your toddler is likely to remain stationary and keep an eye on you. When you are firmly in one spot, then it's his time to wander. He knows where you are and knows he can get to you should he need to. Now he can wander out a bit, perhaps even some distance from you. He may not venture far, perhaps a distance of something less than 200 feet (if you happen to be in a park or other large open area). When he reaches his personal safety threshold, he will probably go no further and will meander back to where you are. This is a built-in logic that enables him to explore safely, comfortable in the knowledge that you are there for him.

If you move to another spot, he may find it unsettling and perhaps even burst into tears. It is your job to go and get

---

safety alert

Your child may not be able to walk steadily or safely for at least a few months. Furthermore – and this is important – his physical abilities have outstripped his awareness of danger. He doesn't look down while he is walking and he may have no sense of the hazards that surround him now that he is mobile. Indeed, he will have little or no memory of something that caused him trouble even earlier that day.

him and bring him to your new spot, from where he will begin exploring again. It is this that makes walking somewhere with him so challenging. He is incapable of really following you and may want to be in the stroller or carried, though just seconds ago, he was full of energy and happily moving around. Take this into consideration when planning an expedition or even just a walk home from the park. Only then can you avoid the anger and frustration that often arises when you are trying to get somewhere quickly.

toddler self-esteem

It isn't only rules and other constraints that may frustrate your toddler. Life is still confusing to him – there are many things that he can't do yet. Some are just too demanding physically; others adults will not allow him to do. As a result, his self-esteem and dignity may suffer. Because he is not as strong nor as coordinated as he wishes to be

TIPS and techniques for helping your toddler gain confidence with his walking

- Give him a ball to throw.

- Play music so that he can use dance movements on the spot.

- Use riding toys such as toy cars with wheels, so that he can move by pushing with his feet.

- As you guide him, let him push his stroller or specially designed toys that can be pushed or pulled without risk of tipping or lurching as he holds on to them.

(nowhere is this more obvious than when he's trying to copy his mom, dad or older sibling), he may struggle to do something he cannot do.

Some frustration, of course, is a good thing since it is the inability to do something that gets your child to try harder, to begin to problem-solve and to learn. But too much frustration and he may give up. Be ready to step in when you notice him becoming increasingly frustrated. By helping him complete the task – don't just do it for him – you can show him how to get past the roadblock next time. Make sure that he is playing with toys that are right for his size and strength. You want him to feel as competent and confident as possible.

POINTS TO REMEMBER

- Toddlers are very active and need a number of small nutritious meals or snacks each day.

- It is not important how early your child begins to stand or cruise, but that he is comfortable and encouraged with each attempt.

- Make sure that your toddler is playing with toys that are right for his size and strength, to enhance his confidence and enjoyment.

your growing preschooler

In this book, the speed and enormity of the physical changes that your child will experience between birth and age two have been discussed a lot. Certainly, the physical changes to come will be much less dramatic than those of this earlier period, but not necessarily less exciting. By the age of three, your child may be helping with simple tasks around the house and will enjoy your praise. By giving it to him freely, you will also give him self-confidence to develop and mature in the years to come.

healthy attitudes toward eating

This period in your child's life shows yet another slowing in weight gain. You should expect a gain of only about five pounds in the third year, while he may grow in height by around three-and-a-half inches. This will slow further in his fourth year, dropping to about four-and-a-half pounds and two-and-a-half inches. He may look thin compared to his earlier, pudgier self, but this is just the natural transition to the slimmer, more muscular years of five and beyond.

Your child will likely be eating a lot as his body continues to grow and change. It is important that you ensure that he is being offered the right amount of proteins, minerals and vitamins. Try to introduce a wide variety of foods to him – and don't give up if he doesn't like it the first time. If you make experimenting with different foods, textures and flavors fun, your child is more likely to become an adventurous eater at a later age.

If he refuses certain foods, try to make sure that the foods he does eat give him the nutrition he needs. You can encourage him to try new foods when he sits down to eat with the whole family. A useful guideline is that there is no food served to your family that your toddler cannot have (unless, of course, your doctor has noted specific allergies). Allow him to experiment with little tastes instead of a full serving on his plate that he must finish. By seeing that you value his opinions and feelings, he will more likely try and enjoy new foods.

physical development

By the time your child reaches the age of three, his appearance has begun to change again. He'll begin to look very different from a toddler. Having grown out of his chubby cheeks, his face is now thinning out. He is longer and more leggy, more graceful and less roly-poly. He may also sound different from a toddler, as his language is developing rapidly. Because of these changes, it is easy to think that your three-year-old is capable of more than he really is. Despite appearing to be able to, he cannot really grasp difficult concepts and consequences. Try not to expect too much too soon. You can help by being patient and supportive.

With his physical changes have come cognitive and other types of development. Your child is better at remembering and, therefore, anticipating and looking forward to things. He may put his boots on (irrespective of whether they are on the right feet or not) or perhaps get his own juice from the fridge (with some unavoidable spills) or "go potty" on his own. These are accomplishments that you ought to encourage.

physical activity and feelings

Preschool children feel "at one" with their bodies and do not separate physical activities from thinking and feeling. This has a number of results. First, when your child discovers that he is unable to do something, he may feel that he is a failure. He is also always challenging himself to see what he can do: how far and how fast he can run, how high he can climb. He needs to do this, for this is how he learns about his abilities as well as how he can do better. Be encouraging and supportive. Don't prevent him from trying (except when he may hurt himself) and allow him to feel exhilarated by his successes and frustrated by his failures. He will learn from both.

Here are a few physical activities that your preschooler may enjoy:

- swimming
- dancing
- bouncing lightweight balls
- tricycle riding – with a helmet
- music and movement (gymnastics) classes
- playing at a park – with supervision
- helping you fetch things within reach at home or at the supermarket
- helping with simple household chores such as sweeping and shoveling (with brooms and shovels geared to his size).

A consequence of the connection between thoughts, feelings and actions is that your child will involve his body as well as his mind in coming to an understanding of the world. He may jump and prance about when happy or excited, and may cry and stamp his feet when frustrated or upset. Some parents try to discourage this, perhaps out of embarrassment, especially when they're in a public place.

But any attempt to separate the physical from feelings may spoil things for him. He may not even find the activity fun if he's not allowed to act out his emotions.

Show your child that you delight in his successes; that you understand his disappointment and that tears are a reasonable response for him to have. And they are, for he is learning to understand his feelings.

Your preschooler is discovering what his body can and cannot do. Having developed to the point where he has reasonable control over his body, he's now ready to use it to learn more. His newfound capacity to imagine and to be creative are matched with a new level of small-muscle dexterity and the ability to create and play using props and tools. Depending on the kind of life he leads – is he home all day or does he have structured groups to which he goes daily? – he will require different kinds of stimuli and structure to round out his experience. It is helpful for you, then, to take stock of what your child's daily routine provides and to make the effort to introduce other activities that will help develop small- and large-muscle coordination.

your child at home

The child who stays at home on a daily basis needs structure and variety. A morning of solitary play while you are occupied with household chores should be followed by some active outdoor play. Because you – or your child's caregiver – are the source of most activities, it is up to you to provide him with new experiences, whether it is listening to music and books on tape or working with new play materials and toys. It is also important for you to help your child to deal with his frustrations when working with new and challenging materials and games. He may not have the patience, for example, to stick to a challenging puzzle by himself, but with your involvement and encouragement, he will overcome his frustration and impatience, and enjoy it more and more.

Never look down to test the ground before taking your next step; only he who keeps his eye fixed on the far horizon will find the right road.

DAG HAMMARSKJÖLD

preschoolers and independence

It is during his preschool years that your child will come to think of himself as an individual. Nowhere is this more obvious than in his awareness of his body and his rights to privacy and autonomy. Of course, it is still your job to make sure that he is healthy, well-fed and clean, but the more you can allow him to take control of his daily routine, the happier he will be. And the more he can learn about both his physical abilities and the responsibilities that come with independence, the more mature he will become. And, maybe best of all, after your preschooler learns these daily tasks, he will be pleased to do them just to show you he can. He may very well become a real "helper" around the house.

Most preschool children want to help in choosing their own clothes when it comes to getting dressed, which they are increasingly able to do. You can make it that much easier by selecting clothes with elastic waists, big buttons, Velcro or oversized zippers. Allow your child to give his input as to which clothes you buy and which he'll wear. Try arranging his drawers so that you will be reasonably happy, no matter what he chooses to put on. There will be less unpleasantness, and he'll feel grown-up by making his own choices. Everybody will be happier.

TIPS and techniques for helping your preschooler develop confidence

- Arrange the house so that it is child-friendly. It is unlikely he will be able to move comfortably and confidently about the house if it is too dark and scary. Keep your rooms and hallways brightly lit or, better yet, install special children's light switch extensions that he can turn on and off himself.

- If you want your child to wash up after playing, make sure he can reach everything he needs in the bathroom without getting into razors, prescriptions and other hazards. In addition, check the temperature of your water at its hottest to make sure that he can't scald himself.

- Install coat hooks at your child's height. You might be able to avoid the arguments about his dropping his coat anywhere when he comes in, and he will likely be very proud of himself for being so grown-up about hanging up his own coat.

- Arrange toy bins or shelves at your child's height for "tidy up" time so that he can put his toys away conveniently.

- Try to buy clothing that is easy for your child to use – for example, Velcro fasteners and large buttons make it easy for him to dress himself.

your child in a play group

Since your child's life in a play group or preschool is likely organized, regimented and physically active, he may need some portion of the day when he can be by himself and do what he enjoys. His experience at home needn't be a whirlwind of new and interesting activities and challenges. Get a sense of the kind of activities he gets at group play and supplement this with other kinds of activity. If, for instance, your child is getting a lot of exercise and running about in his play group, then arts and crafts, listening to music, being read to and some quiet time will be what he enjoys – and needs. If your child is in an all-day program, he will benefit most from having your individual attention. Try to set aside some time every day to be together; having you there with him is what he'll want and enjoy.

TIPS and techniques for playtime and your preschooler

- Arts and Crafts: Making things with his hands is a crucial activity for your child's fine motor development. He wants to learn how to make things work for him. Crayons, scissors, and glue become tools with which he can create. Provide him with the time and equipment so that he can discover what he can do with them.

- Music: The more music your child hears at this age, the more it will mean to him. He will absorb its tunefulness, appreciate its rhythm, dance to it and learn to love it.

- Building: Whether your preschooler uses specially designed educational toys or good old-fashioned blocks, he may enjoy creating and building things with his newfound coordination (and knocking them down) and will learn some essential skills.

- Physical Play: As we said earlier, children at this age involve their whole bodies in activities and are continually pushing the limits. You can encourage this (and his large-motor development) by getting your child to apply some of his new skills to day-to-day activities, whether it's running to answer the phone or using a step stool to get something down from the cupboard for you. He will feel he is being a help and will develop more confidence in himself.

CASE STUDY 4

Early every Saturday morning, four-year-old Joshua and his mother Shari head off to the local farmers' market to do their fruit and vegetable shopping. It is a casual morning of browsing about the market and exploring that both of them love. About six months earlier, Shari had noticed that she and Joshua were often starting the outing with an argument over what he would wear. After only a few of these crack-of-dawn fights, Shari realized she could avoid them entirely if she didn't concern herself too much with how smartly dressed Joshua was.

One weekend, Joshua was allowed to choose whatever he wanted to wear with the one condition: that since it was a chilly day he had to make sure he would be dressed warmly. Not only did Joshua choose wisely and dress himself – with only a little help – he proudly declared all morning, to whomever would listen, that he had dressed himself today and hadn't he done a good job. No one disagreed, despite the mismatched socks and strange color combinations.

body awareness

Some children are self-conscious about their bodies, while others are not. As a parent, you must make room for these individual differences. Even children who had previously not been self-conscious about their bodies may all of a sudden demand some privacy. This is a very natural and healthy reaction. Your child is unlikely to be embarrassed in front of his parents and siblings, yet may not want to be naked, for example, in a public changing area. Respect his request for privacy by providing a towel behind which he can change. This new attitude generally doesn't signify that he has a poor sense of himself and his body, but rather that he wants some privacy. Because you've probably been used to his complete lack of self-consciousness when he was younger, this development may surprise you but may help explain his new need for privacy. He probably associates it with being more grown-up.

Until now, your child tended to assume that all other children's bodies were just like his and that his mother's and father's are different because they are so different altogether from him. Now, when he sees another child naked, he is likely to ask for an explanation. A simple answer labeling body parts will most likely satisfy any curiosity. There is a tendency for adults to make too big a deal out of it, or perhaps to give more information than children likely need. That's why the best approach is to provide as straightforward and simple an answer as the question allows. He is not asking that you explain all the facts of life to him; he just wants to know why he is different from that little girl.

POINTS TO REMEMBER

- Praise your child for his accomplishments — be patient and supportive.

- Make experimenting with new food tastes and textures fun.

- A child who is in preschool or an active play group may have to balance the day with some quiet time.

fitness and fun

healthy attitudes toward fitness

Your baby is born naturally active. From the day that he is born, he wants to move and use his large and small muscles to explore his surroundings. At two or three years of age he will want to run, play, climb, jump and roll. This natural energy and enthusiasm should be channeled into fitness opportunities where your child can have fun, learn about his body, develop confidence and experience interacting with others.

As your child grows, keeping him fit is an important factor to consider. If you model healthy attitudes toward physical activity and fitness early in your child's life, you create the opportunity for future enjoyment and success. Increasing his level of fitness will improve his health as well as help him deal with his day-to-day stress more effectively.

fitness and self-esteem

Being active will also help your child's social development. He will be introduced to situations where he has to solve problems, make decisions, and learn the skills of communication, taking turns and sharing. This can have a significant impact on his feelings of self-worth and self-esteem. When he says "watch me," it is often when he is demonstrating a newfound physical skill.

Children who have positive physical experiences at a young age are more likely to continue participating in physical and sport activities as they grow. By carefully planning age appropriate activities that help your child develop skills and experience success, he will be more likely to feel good about himself.

fitness and play

Your child's earliest motor skills, such as grasping and reaching, are the building blocks for the development of more complex movements. It is important to understand your child's stages of readiness for developing particular motor skills. For example, a child will walk before he runs. However, the age and rate at which a child develops motor skills vary considerably. Children progress through motor sequences at individual speeds. Chronological age is not a good indicator of when a child will develop a skill.

Create an environment that makes him feel as confident as possible. Make sure that the activity is age appropriate and encourage him to be active every day, with a combination of structured and free play.

outdoor play safety alert

Falls and playground accidents are leading causes of pediatric injury. Check the playground for safety and hazardous hard surfaces.

- **Teach children how to use playground equipment safely.**

- **Always supervise children on the playground.**

- **Remove cords and drawstrings on children's hoods, hats and jackets and tuck in all clothing that can get caught on playground equipment.**

- **Practice sun safety — use protective sunscreen and stay out of the midday sun.**

- **Choose an outdoor toy that is suitable for your child's age. Always supervise children playing on riding toys and keep them away from traffic situations.**

CASE STUDY 5

When three-year-old Sean was invited to his cousin Jason's fifth birthday party, he was quite excited. It was summer time, and Jason's parents were having a baseball theme party. When the day finally arrived, Sean woke up early and got ready for the party.

When Sean and his dad arrived at the party, some of the children were already playing ball in the backyard. Sean watched them. After a few minutes, his father came over with a small sponge ball and asked him if he wanted to play catch. His father stood a few feet away from him, and threw the ball, but when Sean reached out with his hands, he couldn't catch it.

After giving Sean some coaching, he threw the ball again and again. He was quite frustrated by his son's inability to catch and he told him to try harder. At this point, he realized that this was not the time or place for Sean to learn how to catch a ball – maybe he wasn't ready – and decided that it would be best to try a different activity.

When the baseball game finally started, most of the children were very excited. Sean was upset and wanted to leave. But his father calmed him down and eventually they joined the other children. His dad suggested that they could help the teams by delivering the refreshments and by watching together, he would learn more about the game.

creating a home activity area

If you have some open space in your home, it is easy to create an indoor play area with a few simple pieces of homemade or purchased equipment.

Make sure the environment and equipment are safe. Remove any throw rugs, as children can easily slip on them. If possible, carpet the whole room, with a little padding underneath. Remove all breakable items from the room, and put safety covers on all electrical outlets.

Equipment used for physical activity does not have to be expensive. Target games can be played with a ball of socks, thrown into a laundry basket; spoons can be thrown into a plastic container; soft objects can be thrown into a circle. Bats can be made with cardboard tubes or rolled up newspaper. Balls can be purchased, or you can scrunch up pieces of paper, use some rolled up socks or small beanbags.

You may consider buying a cloth crawl tube and a large exercise mat for rolling, summersaulting or tumbling. You can also sit on the floor with your child and his friends, and roll various-sized balls back and forth to each other.

If you have a backyard, a safe jungle gym is a great resource for outside play but requires strict supervision. Some are multistation units with swings, monkey bars, and rings. Almost every major muscle group can be exercised on jungle gyms.

A variety of outdoor items can also help your child develop motor skills. Old tires laid together in different patterns make excellent paths for children to walk, run and hop through. The tire swing can be used to swing from, or makes a great target for throwing balls through.

A tetherball set can be a great game for helping your young child to develop eye-hand coordination. Tetherball sets usually include a long pole that is secured into the ground. A cord is attached to the top of the pole and a ball is attached to the other end of the cord. The goal of the game is for your child to hit the ball with a bat or his hands, trying to get the ball to wrap around the pole. The harder the ball is hit, the faster it wraps around the pole. With supervision, two children can play this game at the same time.

Tips and techniques for encouraging physical activity

Parents and siblings are role models for fitness. If your family is active, then your children will probably have more opportunities to explore and experience positive physical activity.

- Teach your child outdoor and indoor physical games.
- Take your child to the playground where he can interact with others in an outdoor setting.
- Create play areas in your home - use pillows, chairs, cardboard boxes, etc.
- Include active games at your child's next party.
- Keep activities appropriate to attention span and age of your child.
- When your child appears to be losing interest in an activity, change or modify the activity.
- Adapt equipment to meet the needs of your child.
- Create opportunities for family fitness activities.

ideas for physical activities

infants

- **Rhymes while changing or dressing your baby**

  While baby is on his back, move his legs either in toward the chest or up and down, and sing the following rhyme:

  > "Moving, moving back and forth,
  > In and out and up and down,
  > I can move my legs around."

- **Baby Jump**

  Using a cushion on your lap, encourage your baby to jump up and down while supporting him under his arms, or by his hands when he is older.

- **Obstacle Crawl**

  Encourage your child to crawl around obstacles and household objects. Have him crawl through your legs, under tables, around chairs, backwards and forwards.

toddlers

- **Roll the Ball**

  Have your child sit opposite you with his legs wide apart in a "V" shape. Sit the same way and roll a soft ball between his legs. He pushes or rolls the ball back to you, trying to land it between your legs. After a few successful rolls, move further apart.

- **Kick the Ball**

  Standing away from your child, kick a large ball to him and have him kick it back to you. Increase the distance after a few successful kicks.

- **Movement and Music**

  Have your child move and dance to the beat of music. When you turn the volume down, have him drop down to a squat or sitting position. When you restart the music, tell him to start moving again.

preschoolers

- **Jump and Turn**

  Have your child jump up and down on the spot. When you clap your hands, have him jump and turn so that he is facing a different direction. You may want to incorporate music or vary the activity. Instead of jumping, have him hop on one foot.

- **Balancing**

  Give your child a marked spot, for example a taped "X" on the floor. While staying on the marked spot, have him balance on one foot at a time, on his toes, etc. Try adding music.

- **Target Practice**

  Using soft household items, such as soft toys, balls of socks or plastic cups, practice target throwing. A laundry basket, wastepaper basket or bucket make good targets. Vary the distance of the toss according to his ability level.

POINTS TO REMEMBER

- Make sure your child's physical activity is suitable for his ability level.

- A physically active child is healthier and develops self-esteem with accomplishments.

- Encourage your child to be physically active by being a role model.

- Check the safety of all play equipment at home, as well as outdoors.

- Each child is different; watch him and encourage him to participate in activities that he enjoys.

summing up

Watching the process of growth and development from newborn to preschool is one of the most exciting rewards of being a parent in the early years. You will likely remember for a lifetime that first smile, those first words and those first steps. The delight you felt as your pudgy baby grew into a leggy preschooler will endure as well.

As a parent, you are a witness to one of the true wonders of nature. And you are much more than that. It is because of you and the care, attention and love that you have provided that this transformation is possible. And it is you who will give your child that essential blend of emotional and nutritional sustenance that will enable him to grow up strong, safe, confident and capable.

centile chart 1
boys' weights

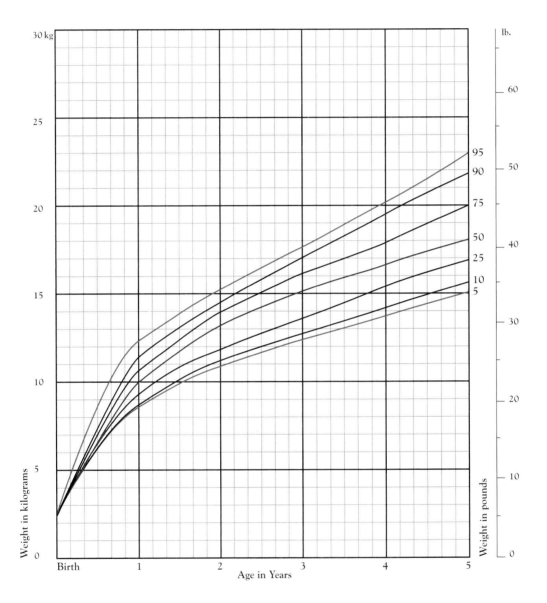

To enter your child's weight and height, find his age at the bottom of the chart, and his height or weight up the side of the chart. Make a mark with a colored pencil or pen where a straight line from his age and a straight line from his height or weight intersect. You can use each chart to monitor more than one child's rate of growth by using a different color for each child.

Note: *The charts on this page and pages 89-91 are adapted from* Your Growing Child: From Babyhood Through Adolescence, *by Penelope Leach, New York: Alfred A. Knopf, 1995.*

centile chart 2
boys' heights

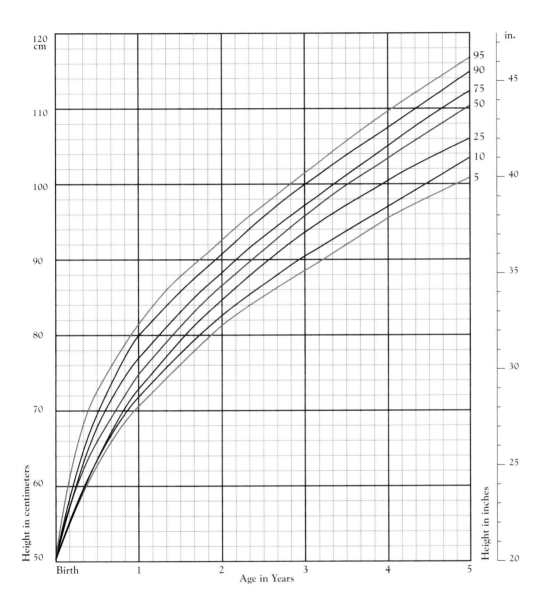

The red line in the middle is the 50th centile, which is the average – 50% of children will weigh or measure more; 50% of children will weigh or measure less.

The two blue lines are the 95th centile at the top and the 5th centile at the bottom, marking the limits of very large and very small children. Almost all children's weights and lengths will be between these lines.

In between there are two more pairs in black lines – the 90th and the 10th (10% of children are bigger or smaller) and the 75th and the 25th (a quarter of children are bigger or smaller).

All these children are within the normal limits, although there is a wide variance between children's weights and heights.

centile chart 3
girls' weights

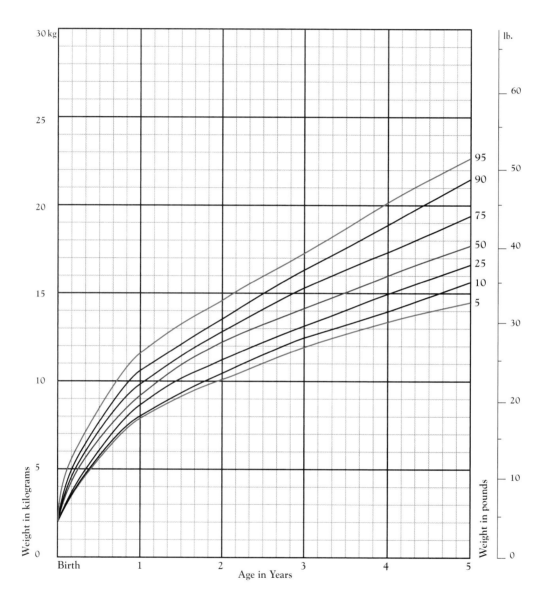

centile chart 4
girls' heights

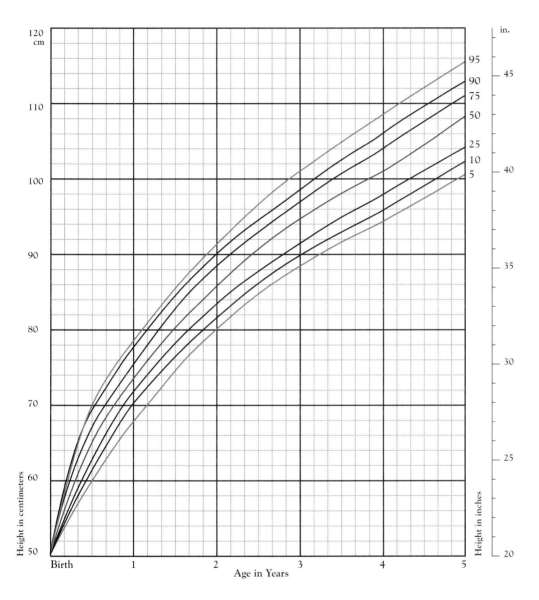

My Child's Growth and Development Record

Fill in the age at which your child first does each of the following activities:

ACTIVITY	AGE	COMMENTS
Lifts head		
Moves hands together		
Rolls over		
Reaches for object		
Passes object from hand to hand		
Sits		
Crawls		
Begins to stand		
Thumb-finger grasp		
"Cruises"		

ACTIVITY	AGE	COMMENTS
Walks		
Scribbles		
Walks up steps		
Jumps		
Pedals tricycle		
Other		

recommended reading

- *Growing Together: A Parent's Guide to Baby's First Year*, by Dr. William Sears, La Leche League International, P.O. Box 1209, Franklin Park, Illinois, 60131-8209 U.S.A., 1998.

- *The Baby Book: Everything You Need to Know about Your Baby – from Birth to Age Two*, by Dr. William Sears and Martha Sears, R.N., New York: Little Brown and Company, 1993.

- *Parenting the Fussy Baby and the High-Need Child*, by Dr. William Sears and Martha Sears, R.N., New York: Little Brown and Company, 1996.

- *Your Baby and Child: From Birth to Age Five*, New version, by Penelope Leach, New York: Alfred A. Knopf, 1998.

- *Your Growing Child: From Babyhood through Adolescence*, by Penelope Leach, New York: Alfred A. Knopf, 1995.

- *Children First: What our society must do – and is not doing – for our children today*, by Penelope Leach, New York: Alfred A. Knopf, 1994.

accreditation

Growth and Development is based on the works of
Dr. William Sears, Martha Sears, R.N. and Dr. Penelope Leach.

Editors: Dali Castro and Carol Lawlor

Designers: The Adlib Group and Beth Gorbet

resources for your child's safety

In Canada:
Infant and Toddler Safety Association (ITSA)
385 Fairway Road South, Suite 4A - 230
Kitchener, Ontario N2C 2N9
(519) 570-0181

In the USA:
Consumer Product Safety Commission (CPSC)
Washington, DC, 20207
(301) 504-0580

The Injury Prevention Program (TIPP) provides
information on accident-proofing your child's environment.
The Family Guide to Car Seats lists all approved car seats.
For information on this and other parenting publications,
send a self-addressed stamped envelope to:
The American Academy of Pediatrics
Department C, P.O. 927
Elk Grove Village, Illinois 60009-0927
www.aap.org

Resources for Parenting Information:
In Canada:
Canadian Institute of Child Health
384 Bank St., Suite 300, Ottawa, Ontario K2P 1Y4
(613) 230-8838
cich@cich.ca

In the USA:
I am Your Child Campaign
For further information on parenting resources in
your state, call (888) 447-3400
www.iamyourchild.org

Look for these Parent**Smart** Books
at leading bookstores and other retail outlets

Positive Discipline

Some of the most challenging situations for parents and their child involve dealing with discipline issues. Starting with the basic premise that discipline starts with love, this book looks at changing discipline needs, as children go through early stages of development.

Topics covered in *Positive Discipline* include:
- how discipline techniques can affect a child's self-esteem
- the characteristics of positive discipline
- handling your own emotions and anger
- the trouble with spanking
- discipline versus punishment
- avoiding tantrums
- why you can't spoil with love
- setting appropriate limits

This book provides parents with eight practical strategies they can use to encourage cooperation from their children, and sets out easy-to-follow techniques for handling various discipline issues, including tantrums, defiance and anger. There are sections that provide guidance on dealing with discipline problems when a child is living part-time with separated or divorced parents, and on how parents can better manage their own anger, to the benefit of their children and parenting partners.

How Your Baby & Child Learns

Most parents want their child to have a love of learning and to do well in school. Recent research now confirms that there is much that parents can do to provide the care and stimulation which enhances learning in the first few years. *How Your Baby & Child Learns* contains information on numerous subjects, including creating a positive learning environment, a baby's early brain development and dealing with children who have special needs.

This book explores the stages of a baby's intellectual development. It provides information, as well as tips and techniques, on how parents can stimulate their child's interest in reading and how learning music also enhances mathematical abilities.

Topics covered in *How Your Baby & Child Learns* include:
- how the brain is hard-wired
- learning social responsibility
- numbers and quantitative thinking
- learning through friends
- talking to your baby
- stimulating a healthy curiosity
- talking and listening
- learning through play
- learning by pretending
- toddlers and television
- reading to your child
- music and learning

This book gives parents the information they need to enhance their child's learning opportunities.

Your Baby and Child's
Emotional and Social Development

New research gives us a better understanding of how babies develop emotionally and socially. This book will give parents new insights into these important developmental processes and things they can do to enhance the long term well-being and feelings of security in their child.

Topics covered in *Emotional and Social Development* include:
- ten strategies for your child's healthy emotional development
- baby's feelings
- what it means when babies cry
- the importance of a baby's gaze
- the child-friendly environment
- the five senses
- toddler socializing
- the parent partnership
- enriching the bond

Readers will learn the timing of emotional development, from the child's initial bonding with the parents, to relating to others outside of the immediate family.

This book is must reading for every parent who is concerned with the emotional and social well-being of their child.

Medical Emergencies & Childhood Illnesses

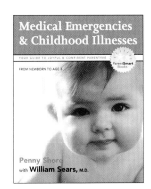

This book should have a place of importance in every home with small children. No matter how carefully children are supervised, medical emergencies can happen. And when they do happen, this guide provides easy-to-follow procedures.

Everything the caregiver needs to know is set out clearly, with instructions on the appropriate course of action. There are three sections in this book: Medical Emergencies, Childhood Illnesses and Your Child's Personal Health Journal. The section on Medical Emergencies covers all of the common situations, including:
- broken or fractured bones
- head and nose injuries
- breathing difficulties
- emergency medical kit
- strains and sprains
- convulsions and seizures
- sunburn
- bites and stings
- choking
- poisoning
- burns
- bleeding
- eye injuries
- shock

A separate section on Childhood Illnesses provides caregivers with an easy-to-understand directory. It includes the symptoms to look for, the action to be taken by the caregiver, as well as an alert on special things to watch for in each particular situation.

The Personal Journal section will provide for an important record of a child's inoculations, illnesses and hospitalizations. It can be used when visiting the family doctor or when traveling.

With children, one thing is certain — illnesses and injuries are inevitable. Having this book conveniently accessible will ensure that information is always available when it is needed.

Joyful and Confident Parenting

This book is essential reading for every new parent. Here is the information and step-by-step advice parents need from the day their new baby joins the family.

Joyful and Confident Parenting addresses the issue of baby bonding with mom and dad as well as others in the extended family, including other caregivers. Readers will learn the steps to help build solid parent-child relationships that will last a lifetime.

The book examines how each member of the family's parenting team can play a meaningful role in the new baby's development. The chapter entitled *Taking Stock* encourages parents to consider their own personal parenting style, the way they were raised by their parents, and how these factors will affect the way they approach the parenting of their own child.

Topics covered in *Joyful and Confident Parenting* include:

- newborn basics
- your parenting style
- baby-proofing your home
- choosing childcare
- creating a support system
- avoiding some parenting pitfalls
- how to achieve positive parenting
- building a healthy parent-child relationship

This book provides parents with the basics of joyful and confident parenting.

The International Advisory Council on Parenting

Penny Shore

Created the *ParentSmart Books* and is President of The Parent Kit Corporation. She was Vice President, Product Development for Hume Publishing, and a management consultant with degrees in psychology and gerontology. An expert on the development of home study programs on a variety of topics, Ms. Shore is a parenting educator and an advocate for effective parenting.

Penelope Leach, Ph.D.

Was educated at Cambridge University, London School of Economics and University of London, where she received her Ph.D. in psychology. She is a renowned author of many books, including *Your Baby and Child* and *Your Growing Child*, fellow of the British Psychological Society, past President of the Child Development Society and acknowledged international expert on the effects of parents' different child-rearing styles on children.

William Sears, M.D.

Regarded as one of North America's leading pediatricians, is a medical and parenting consultant to several magazines and organizations, and a frequent guest on television shows. Dr. Sears received his pediatric training at Harvard Medical School's Children's Hospital and Toronto's Hospital for Sick Children. He is the author of many books on parenting, including *The Baby Book* and *The Discipline Book*.

Martha Sears, R.N.

Is a registered pediatric nurse and co-author, with her husband, William Sears, of many books on parenting, including *Parenting the Fussy Baby and the High-Need Child.* In addition to being a regular contributor to several national magazines for parents, she has appeared on more than a hundred television shows and is a popular speaker at parents' organizations across North America.

Otto Weininger, Ph.D.

Served for 15 years as chairman of the Early Childhood Program at the University of Toronto, where he received his Ph.D. in psychology. He is the author of several books including *Time In* and former editor of *The International Journal of Early Childhood Education*. He is a host and frequent guest on radio and television programs around the world, sharing his expertise on children's education, play, learning and relationships.

YOUR PARENTING JOURNAL

Date   **Comments**

YOUR PARENTING JOURNAL

Date   **Comments**

Date   **Comments**

Date   **Comments**

Date   **Comments**

index